Editor
Jennifer Overend Prior, Ph.D.

Managing Editor
Ina Massler Levin, M.A.

Editor-in-Chief
Sharon Coan, M.S. Ed.

Illustrator
Renée Christine Yates
Bruce Hedges

Cover Artist
Lesley Palmer

Art Coordinator
Kevin Barnes

Art Director
CJae Froshay

Imaging
Temo Parra
Rosa C. See

Product Manager
Phil Garcia

Publishers
Rachelle Cracchiolo, M.S. Ed.
Mary Dupuy Smith, M.S. Ed.

A Year of Language Arts

GRADES 1 - 2

Author

Sarah Kartchner Clark, M.A.

Teacher Created Materials

Teacher Created Materials, Inc.
6421 Industry Way
Westminster, CA 92683
www.teachercreated.com
ISBN-0-7439-3714-7

©2004 Teacher Created Materials, Inc.
Made in U.S.A.

Table of Contents

Introduction

With all the demands of our world, literacy is becoming increasingly vital. Though "literacy" is an often-used word in education today, many children in the world are growing up without a strong literate foundation. Just what is literacy? The dictionary states that a literate person is able to read and write.

The purpose of *A Year of Themes: Language Arts* is to provide a literacy-rich environment in which children learn to use and enjoy written and spoken language. The children will become immersed in print and use their developing language skills in purposeful activities. Students will learn phonetic sounds, hear rhyme and rhythm, and begin to understand language structure. *A Year of Themes: Language Arts* contains familiar stories and nursery rhymes to set a comfortable tone and create a familiar environment.

This book has been divided into nine units—one for each month of the traditional school year. Each segment is based on a theme and has a literature selection and a letter/sound focus. Each segment in this book is organized to include some or all of the following activities:

- lesson plans
- related literature suggestions
- word matching
- learning centers
- phonics activities
- journal writing ideas
- exposure to nonfiction text
- reproducible little books
- creative writing ideas
- group discussion
- art projects
- story-related visual aids
- drama activities
- handwriting

Language Arts Standards and Objectives

All educators should be accountable for teaching skills and objectives that will promote literacy. Listed below are the objectives and skills that are taught in this book.

- Identify characters in a story and retell stories in sequence.
- Identify main characters.
- Predict elements and events in a story.
- Use phonetic skills to decode simple words.
- Identify consonant sound/symbol relationships in the context of words.
- Demonstrate an understanding of print concepts (i.e. pictures, letters, words, book handling, directionality).
- Derive meaning from picture clues, illustrations and using sound/symbol relationships.
- Relate a narrative or creative story by drawing, telling, and writing.
- Spell simple words.
- Write/copy the 26 letters of the alphabet.
- Apply letter/sound relationships as emergent writers.
- Follow simple directions.
- Share ideas, information, opinions, and questions.
- Listen and respond to stories, poems, and nonfiction.
- Participate in group discussions.

A Year of Themes in Language Arts

This book is divided into nine sections, providing you with a different theme and literature selection for each month of the traditional school year. Use the themes to teach skills and information and use the literature selections to teach literacy and mathematical concepts. Here is a suggested outline:

September—A Strong Foundation

The theme this month is A Strong Foundation. Use "The Three Little Pigs" as an opportunity to discuss how important it is to get a good start in the school year. Teach students the rules in your classroom that will make them successful. Discuss how the three pigs chose different materials and therefore had different results. Use this unit to teach the sounds of short *i*, *l*, and *h*.

October—Spiders

October is a good time to use spiders as a theme to teach your students about these crawly creatures. "Little Miss Muffet" has an experience of her own with a spider. Use this unit to introduce the letters *s*, *m*, and short *o*.

November—Pumpkins

Autumn brings the changes of colors and pumpkins on the vine. A pumpkin theme can help your students get ready for fall. Use the unit centered around the poem, "Peter, Peter, Pumpkin Eater" to discover pumpkins and their characteristics. Letters this month are *p*, *k*, and *v*.

December—Gingerbread

What are the holidays without gingerbread? The gingerbread theme lends itself easily to gearing up for the exciting days ahead. "The Gingerbread Man" story adds to the wonder of the season. Use this unit to introduce the sounds of short *a*, *f*, and *x*.

January—Personal Safety

Personal safety is always a concern, but with the snow and the rain, a reminder of how to keep our bodies safe is appropriate. You may even choose to invite professionals in the community that help keep people safe (police officers, fire fighters, etc.), to speak with your class. Use the poem "Jack and Jill" to teach these safety rules and to introduce the letters *j*, *w*, and *d*.

February—Bears

In the dead of winter, many bears are still hibernating. While the bears are busy sleeping, you and your students can study the furry animals. "The Three Bears" unit can help teach the difference between reality and make-believe as well as introduce the letters *b* and *z*.

March—Helping Hands

It's never too soon to teach the lesson of helping others. Use the story "The Little Red Hen" to teach the importance and the benefits of helping others. Look for ways to help others around your school and provide students with these experiences. This unit will introduce the letter sounds of *r*, short *e*, and *n*.

April—Stars

Have you ever looked up at the sky and wondered about the stars and planets? This unit will get your students doing the same. Use the famous poem, "Twinkle, Twinkle, Little Star" to explore the wonders of the night sky. This unit will also introduce the letter sounds of *t*, *y*, and short *u*.

May—Gardens

"Mary, Mary, Quite Contrary" lends itself easily to a theme of gardens and gardening. With spring in the air, it's time to get students planting and learning about successful gardening. What makes a seed grow? Use this unit to teach the letters *q*, *c*, and *g*.

Preparing this Literacy Unit

Encouraging literacy can be a continuous process filling every waking minute. Listed below are activities and suggestions you can implement to make the *A Year of Themes: Language Arts* a success in your classroom.

Making the Little Books

There are nine well-known stories and poems used to teach literacy in this book. Each story or poem comes with a little book for your students. Reproduce the pages of the little book. Books may be assembled before the lesson or students may help complete the following steps. 1. Cut on the lines. 2. Check to make sure the pages are in the correct order. 3. Then staple the pages together. Students may use crayons or colored pencils to color their little books. Be sure to allow time for students to read them independently, with partners, or as a class. When you have finished studying the books in class, send them home for students to share with their families.

Activity Pages

There are activity pages to go with each story. These activity pages are used to give students practice in writing, sequencing, drawing, comprehension, and spelling. Reproduce the activity pages for the students as needed. Directions for using the activity pages are provided in the lesson plans. You will find pages introducing the focus letters and sounds for that unit. This book teaches the lowercase letters, but if time permits, you can add the uppercase letters as well. In addition, this book teaches the short-vowel sounds. If time permits, you may also add the long-vowel sounds.

Literacy Journals

Reading the familiar stories and poems in this book can provide many opportunities for students to reflect on their own lives and experiences. Set aside time for students to "write" and record in their journals. They can express their thoughts and ideas through pictures and words. Write a question on the chalkboard for students to respond to in their journals. You can quickly make a literacy journal by stapling lined sheets of paper inside two sheets of construction paper. Encourage students to design pictures for the covers. Once students have responded to the questions in their journals, be sure to allow them to share what they have written and drawn with you and others in the class.

Word Wall

Set aside a place in your classroom to write down easy-to-read, common words that are found in the little books. Allow students to practice reading these words before and after they read the little books. Encourage students to add words they think need to be on the word wall.

On the Look Out

Encourage students to look for information related to the topics being studied. Students may find newspaper articles, magazine articles, letters, books, stories, etc. Bring in any kind of information that appropriately teaches and addresses the themes taught. Share and discuss these as a class, and post them for future reference.

The Three Little Pigs

One pig built his house of straw.

Oh, no! Oh, no!

One pig built his house of sticks.

Oh, no! Oh, no!

One pig built his house of bricks.

Smart pig! Smart pig!

Then the wolf came to blow them down.

Huff, puff! Huff, puff!

Down went the houses of straw and sticks.

Huff, puff! Huff, puff!

But he couldn't blow down that house of bricks.

Huff, puff! Huff, puff!

Who's afraid of the big, bad wolf?

Not us! Not us!

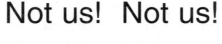

The Three Little Pigs Lesson Plans

Week One

1. Bring in samples of bricks, straw, and sticks. Ask your class to identify these items. What could a person do with them? As a class, brainstorm and record options on the chalkboard. Then explain that you are going to read a story about what three animals did with these items.

2. Read the story "The Three Little Pigs." You may copy and enlarge page 6 to use for this activity. As you read the story aloud, encourage your students to join in on the repetitive parts, "Oh, no! Oh, no!" and "Huff, puff! Huff, puff!"

3. Discuss with students what the pigs did with the bricks, straw, and sticks. Which house was the strongest? Why? Ask students why it is important to have a strong and sturdy house. Discuss materials used in houses built in their neighborhoods.

4. Distribute copies of "The Three Little Pigs" little book. Have students color the pages of this book, cut them out, and staple the books together. Pair students with partners and have them read their books together.

Week Two

1. Discuss the sounds for letters *i* (short *i*), *l*, and *h*. Introduce the sounds that these letters make. Explain that sometimes these sounds are found at the beginning, the middle, or at the end of a word. Make a story chart of page 6 and have students locate words that have these focus letters in them, such as *pig*, *house*, *bricks*, *sticks*, *little*, *his*, and *huff*. Encourage students to share other words not found in the story that use these letter sounds. Have students complete page 12 for reinforcement.

2. Read "The Three Little Pigs" aloud to students as they follow along in their little books. Point to each word as you read it. After reading the story, have students look for words. Write the word *pig* on the chalkboard and ask students to find and point to the word. Also, have the students find *house*, *huff*, *no*, *straw*, *sticks*, *bricks*, *built*, *not*, *us*. Discuss how illustrations and pictures can help to locate words. Have students complete page 13.

3. Ask the students to retell the story of "The Three Little Pigs" to check comprehension. Make up parts of the story that do not exist to see if students can correct you. Also, tell parts of the story out of sequence and have students correct your sequencing.

4. Before class, make a list of questions about the story and write them on strips of paper. Place these strips in a bowl. Invite students to select a strip of paper from the bowl and read the questions about the story. Then have students answer the questions. They can ask classmates for help, if needed. Questions might include:

   • Did the wolf eat the three little pigs?

   • Why was the pig that built his house of bricks smart?

   • Why couldn't the wolf blow down the house of bricks?

   • What did the pigs use to build a house?

   • How many pigs were there?

The Three Little Pigs Lesson Plans *(cont.)*

Week Three

1. Explain to the students that you would like to help them have a good school year. Just like the third little pig had a strong house, students need to have a strong classroom. Discuss how important it is to have a classroom where everyone feels comfortable, happy, and safe. This type of classroom can be created with guidelines and rules that everyone follows. Brainstorm and guide students in writing a list of rules where everyone will feel happy and safe. When completed, write these rules on a large piece of paper and have students sign their names at the bottom showing their commitment to follow the rules. Then read each of the rules and have students dramatize them.

2. Read "The Three Little Pigs" to the students. Next, read a different version of "The Three Little Pigs." (See the bibliography on page 96.) Discuss the similarities and differences between the stories. Ask students if these stories are real or make-believe. Have them complete page 14 to determine which animals are real and which are make-believe.

3. Write lines of the story on different sentence strips. Post the sentence strips out of order on the chalkboard. Have students assist you in placing the strips in sequence. Read the sentences again to check the sequence. Make changes as needed.

4. Read the story again with the students while they follow along in their little books. Point to each word as you read it, but do not say all the words. Point to a word without reading it and have students read for you. Allow them to do more and more of the reading each time.

5. As an art activity, supply students with craft sticks and glue. They can design a house by gluing the sticks together. When the houses are complete, make construction paper available to students to make three little pigs and a big bad wolf. Students can act out the story using their props.

Week Four

1. Discuss whether the pigs and the wolf in the story are real or make-believe characters. How can you tell? Allow time for students to explain their answers. Then discuss the types of homes where real animals live. Bring in a collection of posters, books, and magazine pictures of animal homes. Distribute copies of page 15 to the students. Have students match the animals and their homes.

2. Share the unusual version of the story, *The True Story of the Three Little Pigs*. (See the bibliography, page 96.) Discuss the differences between the stories. Encourage students to think of similar stories. Have children dictate a similar story for you. Write the stories and have students illustrate them. Make covers for these little books and store them in the class library.

3. As a concluding activity for this unit, have students work in groups of four or five to dramatize the story. Invite one student to be the narrator. Give students time to prepare their stories and to gather props. Students may use props found in the classroom or bring in items from home. Share the skits with the class or with another class.

Literacy in the Works

This page provides learning center suggestions that can be used to reinforce skills taught and discussed in the classroom. Select the centers that you think would best meet the needs of your students.

Reading Center

- On each of several sentence strips write the lines from "The Three Little Pigs." At this center, have students work together to read the sentences and determine the sequence of the story. Have a little book of this story available for students to check their work.

- Set up an area in your room (complete with large beanbags, pillows, and chairs) for independent reading. Keep a shelf of books available at all times for students to read and browse. For this center, have versions of "The Three Little Pigs" available for students to read and compare. (See the bibliography on page 96.)

Art Center

- Set up an easel with paper. Have students use watercolors to paint pictures of the three pigs or other scenes from the story. Display the illustrations around the room when the paintings are dry.

Writing Center

- Provide paper and writing utensils for students to write letters to or draw pictures of one of the characters in the story. Students may choose to write letters to one of the pigs or to the wolf. When finished, have each student place his or her letter in an envelope and attach a sticker for a stamp. Students can place their letters in a classroom mailbox. (You may want to respond to student letters.)

Science Center

- Display nonfiction books, magazine articles, and posters about pigs and wolves. Have students browse the materials to learn more about these animals. Arrange a time in the day to have students report to the class what they have learned about the animals and how they live.

Math Center

- Provide building materials such as nuts, bolts, screws, nails, etc. Have students categorize each of these items into groups and then have students count the groups. Which group has the most items? Which group has the fewest? How are these building materials used to build houses?

Dramatic Play Center

- Make a variety of building materials available for students to use to build their own houses. Materials might include toothpicks, craft sticks, blocks, plastic interconnecting blocks, straw, sticks, cardboard, paper, and rocks. Have students build houses with these materials. Once the houses have been built, have students "huff and puff" to blow the houses down. Which of the materials made the sturdiest houses? Which houses came down easily? In which house would you like to live? Which house was the easiest to build? Which house took the most time to build? Which materials would students suggest the three little pigs use? Why?

Making the Little Book

The Three Little Pigs

1

One pig built his house of straw. Oh, no! Oh, no!

2

One pig built his house of sticks. Oh, no! Oh, no!

3

One pig built his house of bricks. Smart pig! Smart pig!

4

Making the Little Book (cont.)

Then the wolf came to blow them down. Huff, puff! Huff, puff! 5

Down went the houses of straw and sticks.
Huff, puff!
Huff, puff! 6

But he couldn't blow down that house of bricks.
Huff, puff!
Huff, puff! 7

Who's afraid of the big, bad wolf?
Not us! Not us! 8

Letters and Sounds

Practice writing each letter below two times. Draw a picture that has that letter sound in it.

i = p<u>i</u>g   l = <u>l</u>ittle   h = <u>h</u>uff

i   i

_____   _____
- - - - - - - - - - - - - - - - - - - -
_____   _____

l   l

_____   _____
- - - - - - - - - - - - - - - - - - - -
_____   _____

h   h

_____   _____
- - - - - - - - - - - - - - - - - - - -
_____   _____

12   ©Teacher Created Materials, Inc.

Word Matching

These letter sounds come from the story "The Three Little Pigs." Read the word and then write the word. Draw a picture that goes with the word.

1. l̲ittle _____

2. p̲i̲g _____

3. h̲ouse _____

4. b̲ricks _____

5. h̲is _____

Real or Make-Believe?

Do the pictures show animals doing real or make-believe things? Draw circles around the pictures that show animals doing real things. Draw Xs across the pictures that show animals doing make-believe things.

1.

2.

3

4.

5

6.

Draw a picture of an animal that is doing something make-believe. Share your silly picture with your classmates.

Animal Homes

Pigs don't really live in houses but animals live in homes. Draw a line from each animal to its home.

Little Miss Muffet

Little Miss Muffet

Sat on a tuffet,

Eating her curds and whey.

Along came a spider,

Who sat down beside her,

And frightened Miss Muffet away.

Spiffy Spider Information

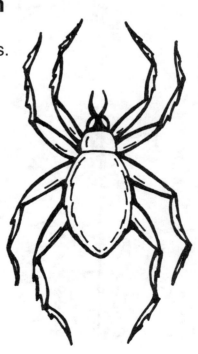

- There are more than 30,000 different kinds of spiders.

- Spiders are arachnids.

- Spiders live in forests, deserts, gardens, swamps, mountains, and fields.

- Spiders have eight legs and two main body parts.

- Spiders have very strong skin.

- Spiders do not have backbones.

- Spiders lay eggs.

- Spiders are helpful. They eat harmful insects.

- Some spiders are poisonous to people.

Little Miss Muffet Lesson Plans

Week One

1. If possible, display a spider in a jar for students to observe. Have students share their observations of what they notice about the spider. What does it look like? How do they think it would feel? What do they think this spider eats? How old do they think the spider is?

2. On the chalkboard, draw three columns. In the first column, write all the information that students already know about spiders. In the second column, write questions they have. At the end of the lesson, record the information that students have learned in the third column.

3. Read and discuss the facts about spiders on page 16. Ask students what they would do if a spider came down next to them while they were eating their lunches. Explain that you have a poem about a little girl who had that experience. Make a large chart of the poem on page 16. Read the poem "Little Miss Muffet" aloud.

4. Distribute copies of the "Little Miss Muffet" little book. Have students color the pages and then cut them out. Help students assemble and staple their books together. Divide students into pairs and have them read their little books together.

Week Two

1. Discuss the sounds of letters *s*, *m*, and short *o*. Introduce the sounds that these letters make. Explain to students that sometimes these sounds are found at the beginning, the middle, or the end of a word. Using the chart you made of page 16, have students locate words that have these letters in them. Some examples include *Miss*, *Muffet*, *on*, *spider*, *along*. Encourage students to share other words not found in the story that use these letter sounds. Have students complete page 22 for reinforcement of these letters.

2. Read the poem "Little Miss Muffet" aloud to students from a little book like theirs. Have students follow along in their books. Point to each word as you read it. After reading the story, have students look for words. Write the word *Miss* on the chalkboard and see if students can find and point to the word. Other words to look for are *little*, *sat*, *on*, a *tuffet*, *eating*, *along*, *came*, *spider*, *sat*, *beside*. Discuss how illustrations and pictures can help with locating words. Have students complete page 23, using words from "Little Miss Muffet."

3. Have students retell the poem of "Little Miss Muffet" to check comprehension. Make up parts of the story that do not exist to see if students can correct you. Also, suggest an event that takes place out of sequence and have students correct your sequencing.

4. Explain to students that there are some new and difficult words that can be found in the poem. Instruct them to use the pictures to help them determine the meaning of these words. Discuss the following definitions with your students:

   • **tuffet**—a low seat (like a stool)

   • **curds**—the coagulated part of soured milk. Curds are used in the process of making cheese. (Show students cottage cheese. Cottage cheese is similar to the curds and whey Miss Muffet eats.)

   • **whey**—the watery part that separates from the curd is the whey. (Show students the watery part at the top of a carton of yogurt.)

Little Miss Muffet Lesson Plans *(cont.)*

Week Three

1. Read "Little Miss Muffet" aloud again. As the class reads, have two students dramatize the poem. Have one student sit on a small stool eating from a bowl, while another student dangles a pretend spider next to him or her.

2. Cut up slips of paper and place them in a bowl. On each slip, write a line from the poem. Have students each select a slip of paper from the bowl and read the line. As a class, see if you can put the poem in order. The first student in the line is the student with the slip that reads, "Little Miss Muffet sat on a tuffet." Then have the next student line up and continue until students are in the correct order. Have them read their slips again one after another. Make changes as needed. Instruct students to complete the sequencing activity on page 24.

3. Read *The Very Busy Spider*, by Eric Carle (see the bibliography on page 96) and other stories about spiders to your students. Discuss these stories and the role the spiders play in each one. Are the spiders good or bad in the stories?

4. Read the poem again with the students while they follow along in their little books. Point to each word as you read it, but this time, do not say all the words. Point to a word without reading it and have students read it for you. Allow students to do more and more of the reading each time.

5. As an art activity, cut a black construction paper headband for each student. Then cut eight black strips to make the legs of the spiders. They can fold the legs accordion style. To attach the legs, spread paste on one end of each black strip. Attach four legs to one side of the headband. Attach the other four legs to the other side. Secure the headband with tape or a staple in the back.

Week Four

1. Discuss whether Little Miss Muffet and the spider in the story are real or make-believe characters. How can you tell? Allow time for students to explain their answers. Discuss what the spider in the story is doing. Is the spider trying to eat Little Miss Muffet's curds and whey? Then discuss experiences that students have had with spiders. Bring in a collection of posters, books, and magazine pictures that show pictures or stories about spiders.

2. On the chalkboard write, "The spider is…." Have students copy these words and then add an ending to the sentence. Remind them to write a period at the end of the sentence. Provide crayons or colored pencils and have students illustrate their sentences. Have a sharing time for students to share their sentences. Bind student pages together to create a book. Make a cover for this book and store it in the class library. Be sure to read the story aloud with students.

3. As a concluding activity, have a cooking day to let students experience curds and whey. Use the recipes on page 25 to cook in the classroom. Be sure to have parent helpers available. Divide students into groups and let each group make one of the recipes. Be sure to have cooking utensils and other materials available for each group. Have students taste and rate the recipes. Do curds and whey taste good? Did curds and whey taste the way you thought they would? Why or why not? Have a vote to see which recipe is the class favorite.

Literacy in the Works

This page provides learning center suggestions that can be used to reinforce skills taught and discussed in the classroom. Select the centers that you think would best meet the needs of your students.

Science Center

- Have students go with an adult on a nature walk looking for spiders or spider webs. What do students see in the webs? Display nonfiction books, magazine articles, and posters about spiders. Have students browse through these materials to learn more. Arrange a time in the day to have them report to the class what they have learned about spiders.

- Have a spider (where students can not gain access) on display. Students can use a magnifying glass to make close-up observations. Have students quietly discuss and observe the spider with other classmates at this center. What information can they gather from their observations? Do they know what type of spider it is? What makes the spider scary? Why do we think of spiders around Halloween time?

Reading Center

- Have a variety of nursery rhyme books available for students to look at and read. See if students can locate "Little Miss Muffet" in the book. Are the words the same? Are the pictures the same? Compare the similarities and differences.

- Set up an area in your room (complete with large beanbags, pillows, and chairs) for independent reading. Keep a shelf of books available at all times for students to read and browse. For this center, have fictional books about spiders. What do the spiders in these stories do? Are people or other animals afraid of them?

Art Center

- Using yarn and a paper plate, have each student weave a spider web. Cut slits along the sides of the paper plate ahead of time. Students can weave a web by attaching the yarn to the slits in the side of the plate. Have plastic spiders available for students to attach to their webs when finished.

Writing Center

- Supply paper, crayons, and other materials needed for each student to write a poem about a spider. Students may draw pictures in place of words, if necessary. Allow the use of the "Little Miss Muffet" poem as a guide.

Math Center

- Have students draw pictures of spiders on pieces of paper. When finished, have them count all the spider legs on the page and write the number at the top.

Dramatic Play Center

- Have props available for students to act out the poem, "Little Miss Muffet." You need a little stool, a bowl, spoon, and a plastic spider attached to string or yarn. You may choose to have a little hat for "Miss Muffet" to wear.

Little Miss Muffet

1

Little Miss Muffet

2

sat on a tuffet,

3

eating her curds and whey.

4

Making the Little Book *(cont.)*

Along came a spider, 5

and sat down beside her, 6

and frightened Miss Muffet away! 7

The End 8

Letters and Sounds

Three of the letter sounds found in "Little Miss Muffet" are *s, m,* and short *o.*
Review these sounds with students. Have students practice writing the letter two
times below. Then have each student draw a picture of something that has the
same letter sound in it.

s = <u>s</u>pider   m = <u>m</u>iss   o = <u>o</u>n

s   s

m   m

o   o

Word Matching

These words come from the poem "Little Miss Muffet." First, read the word.
Then write the word. Write a sentence using the word. In each box, draw a
picture that goes with the sentence.

1. l<u>i</u>ttle

2. <u>s</u>at

3. <u>o</u>n

4. <u>m</u>uffet

5. <u>s</u>pider

Story Sequencing

Color the pictures below. Cut along the dotted lines. Glue the pictures in the boxes to retell the poem "Little Miss Muffet."

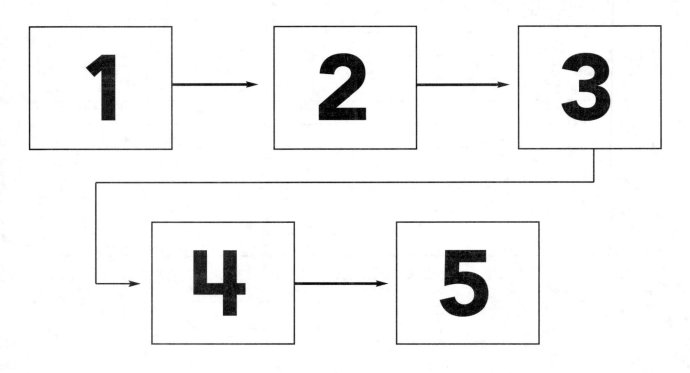

24

Curds and Whey

Materials

- measuring spoons and cups
- recipes
- hot pads
- casserole dish
- serving spoons
- bowls and spoons for each student
- oven
- parent helpers

Cheese and Fruit

Ingredients

- cottage cheese
- strawberries, sliced
- pineapple tidbits
- bananas, sliced
- blueberries
- apples, chopped

Directions

Serve cottage cheese with a variety of fruit. Wash and prepare fruit. Top cottage cheese with fruit pieces. (Be sure to check for food allergies before serving.)

Cheesy Noodles

A delicious cheesy dish!

Ingredients

- egg noodles, 8 oz. (225 g)
- 2 cups (½ L) sour cream
- 1½ cups (375 mL) cottage cheese
- 1 teaspoon (5 mL) salt
- 1½ teaspoons (7 mL) chopped parsley
- 2 tablespoons (30 mL) butter or margarine
- ½ cup (125 mL) grated cheddar cheese
- paprika

Directions

Cook and drain egg noodles. Mix the noodles with sour cream, cottage cheese, salt, and chopped parsley. Place into greased casserole dish. Top with pats of butter, and bake for 30 minutes at 350 degrees F (190° C). When done, top with cheddar cheese, butter or margarine, and a little paprika. Place in oven until cheese topping melts. (Be sure to check for food allergies before serving.)

Peter, Peter, Pumpkin Eater

Peter, Peter, Pumpkin Eater,

Had a wife and couldn't keep her.

He put her in a pumpkin shell,

And there he kept her very well.

• •

Pumpkin Facts

• Pumpkins originally came from Central America.

• It used to be that pumpkins were used as the crust of the pie instead of the filling.

• Pumpkins are used as animal feed.

• The world's largest pumpkin weighed 1,061 pounds.

• Pumpkins are used to make soups, pies, and breads.

• The largest pumpkin pie ever made was over five feet in diameter and weighed over 350 pounds. It contained 80 pounds of cooked pumpkin, 36 pounds of sugar, 12 dozen eggs and took six hours to bake.

• Pumpkins range in size from less than a pound to over 1,000 pounds.

• Pumpkins are made up of mostly water (about 90%).

Peter, Peter, Pumpkin Eater Lesson Plans

Week One

1. Bring in a pumpkin and set it in the center of your class. Ask your class to identify what it is and what we do with it. Brainstorm and record options on the chalkboard. Then explain that you are going to read a story about what a man did with a pumpkin. Before class, make a poster of the poem on page 26. Read the poem with your students. Discuss what Peter did with the pumpkin. What do they think of what he did?

2. Read the poem again, but this time, have students look for rhyming words (*Peter/eater, shell/well*) in the text. Brainstorm with students other words that rhyme with words from the poem like: *Peter, well, had, her,* and *eater*. Discuss unfamiliar words and answer students' questions.

3. Discuss with students why they think Peter put his wife in a pumpkin shell. Why couldn't he keep her? Ask if they have ever seen someone put in a pumpkin shell. How big would this pumpkin need to be? Discuss the absurdity or silliness of the idea. Brainstorm other silly things Peter might do.

4. Distribute copies of "Peter, Peter Pumpkin Eater" little book. Have students color the pages, cut them out, and staple their books together. Pair students with partners and have them read their little books together.

Week Two

1. Discuss the sounds for letters *p, k,* and *v*. Introduce the sounds that these letters make. Explain that sometimes these sounds are found at the beginning, in the middle, or at the end of a word. Display the poem on page 26 on chart paper and have students locate words that have the letters *p, k,* and *v*. Some examples include *Peter, pumpkin, put, kept, keep,* and *very*. Encourage them to share other words not found in the story that use these letter sounds. Have students complete page 32 for reinforcement of these letters.

2. Read "Peter, Peter, Pumpkin Eater" aloud to students from a little book like theirs. Have students follow along in their little books. Model how to point to each word as you read it. After reading the story, have students look for words. Write the word *pumpkin* on the chalkboard and ask students to point to the word. Have students find other words, such as *wife, shell, well, kept, her,* and *there*. Discuss how illustrations and pictures can help with locating words. Have students complete page 33 using words from "Peter, Peter, Pumpkin Eater."

3. Before class, make a list of questions about the story and write them on strips of paper. Place the strips in a bowl. Invite students to select strips from the bowl. Help students read the questions about the poem. Then have them answer the questions.

Peter, Peter, Pumpkin Eater Lesson Plans *(cont.)*

Week Three

1. Discuss things that can be done with pumpkins. What can you put on top of a pumpkin? What could go underneath a pumpkin? What could you put inside a pumpkin? Discuss the possibilities with your class. When finished with this discussion, have students complete page 34 about position words.

2. Read "Peter, Peter Pumpkin Eater" to the students. Next, read a version of the story *Cinderella*. (See the bibliography on page 96.) Discuss the similarities and differences between the two stories that each feature a pumpkin. Ask if these stories are real or make-believe. Read other stories that have pumpkins in them. Discuss whether these stories are real or make-believe.

3. Read the poem again with the students while they follow along in their little books. Point to each word as you read it, but this time, do not say all the words. Point to a word without reading it and have students read it. Allow students to do more and more of the reading each time.

4. As an art activity, supply students with a small pumpkin and paints. Have each student paint a design or a face on his or her pumpkin. Once the pumpkins have dried, they can be displayed on student desks or tables. These pumpkins can become pumpkin pals. Students can write letters to their pals, do projects with them, or show their pals things they are learning in the classroom.

Week Four

1. Discuss the color of pumpkins. How do you make the color orange? Provide students with red, yellow, and blue paint. Allow them to experiment in order to determine how to make the color orange by mixing paints. Once students realize that red and yellow make orange, have them try to make it on their own using a red and yellow crayon.

2. Do a hands-on activity with your class. Bring four or five large pumpkins to class and write numbers on the sides of the pumpkins. Have students toss a hula-hoop over pumpkins and add up the scores. As a variation, write words or letters on pumpkins and ask students to "ring" the pumpkin with a particular word or letter on it.

3. As a concluding activity for this unit, cook different kinds of food using pumpkins. (See the recipes on page 35.) Be sure to have all materials ready and have plenty of parental help on that day. Make arrangements to use an oven at the school. Discuss which part of the pumpkin has been used to make each of the recipes.

Literacy in the Works

This page provides learning center suggestions that can be used to reinforce skills taught. Select the centers that you think would best meet the needs of your students.

Reading Center

- Write the lines of "Peter, Peter, Pumpkin Eater" on different sentence strips. At this center, have students work together to read the sentences and determine the sequence of the poem. Have a little book of this story available for students to check their work.

- Set up an area in your room (complete with large beanbags, pillows, and chairs) for independent reading. Keep a shelf of books available at all times for students to read and browse. For this center, display books about pumpkins. These can be stories that have pumpkins in them or they can be nonfiction books about pumpkins and their characteristics.

Art Center

- Give each student a sheet of white paper. Supply students with pieces of orange, yellow, and green tissue paper and glue. Students then glue the pieces of tissue paper down in the shape of a pumpkin. Have them use yellow for the eyes and the mouth, green for the stem, and the orange for the shape of the pumpkin. Display these around the classroom.

Writing Center

- Provide students with paper and writing utensils and have them each write a letter or draw a picture for Peter (the pumpkin eater), telling him why he shouldn't keep his wife in a pumpkin shell. When finished, have students place their letters in envelopes and attach stickers for stamps. Students can place their letters in a classroom mailbox. (If time permits, you may respond to student letters.)

Science Center

- Display a pumpkin at this center. Cut the top off and allow students to explore the pumpkin with their hands or spoons. Have students use their senses to explore the pumpkin. What do they hear? What do they smell? What does it feel like? How do they think it tastes?

Math Center

- Distribute dried pumpkin seeds (see recipe on page 35) for counting and estimation activities. Match seeds to other manipulatives such as Unifix cubes for set-to-set correspondence. Write numbers on pieces of paper and have students count out that number of pumpkin seeds and glue them to the paper.

Dramatic Play Center

- Have props available and encourage students to dramatize "Peter, Peter, Pumpkin Eater." You can get a large box (such as a refrigerator box) and paint it orange to represent the pumpkin. Be sure to display a poster of the poem so students can refer to it as they act it out.

Making the Little Book

Peter, Peter, Pumpkin Eater

1

Peter, Peter,
pumpkin eater

2

had a wife,

3

and couldn't keep her.

4

Making the Little Book *(cont.)*

He put her in . . .   5

a pumpkin shell.   6

And there he kept her very well!   7

The End   8

Letters and Sounds

Practice writing each letter below two times. Draw a picture that has that letter sound in it.

p = pumpkin   k = keep   v = very

p

_____

- - - - - - - - - - - - - -

_____

p

_____

- - - - - - - - - - - - - -

_____

k

_____

- - - - - - - - - - - - - -

_____

k

_____

- - - - - - - - - - - - - -

_____

v

_____

- - - - - - - - - - - - - -

_____

v

_____

- - - - - - - - - - - - - -

_____

Word Matching

These words come from the poem "Peter, Peter, Pumpkin Eater." First read the word. Then write the word. Read each sentence. Draw a line under the word in the sentence.

1. very
_____
I am very happy.

2. kept
_____
He kept the dog.

3. keep
_____
Can she keep it?

4. Peter
_____
Peter is nice.

5. pumpkin
_____
It is a big pumpkin.

6. put
_____
Jill put it down.

Top, Bottom, In, and Out

Follow the directions in each sentence.

1. Draw a circle on top of the pumpkin.

2. Draw a line below the cat.

3. Draw a girl in the box.

4. Draw a bird in the nest.

Pumpkins, Pumpkins, Pumpkins

Roasted Pumpkin Seeds

Materials and Ingredients

- knife
- 1 small pumpkin
- spoon
- large bowl
- medium bowl
- 2 T. vegetable oil
- salt
- cookie sheet

Cut the pumpkin open. Use a spoon to remove the seeds from the pumpkin and transfer them to a large bowl. Separate the seeds from the pumpkin fiber. Preheat the oven to 350 degrees Fahrenheit (190 degrees Celsius). Place the pumpkin seeds into a medium bowl and toss with oil and a sprinkle of salt. Spread the seeds on a cookie sheet and bake for 30 to 40 minutes or until slightly brown.

Pumpkin Muffins

Materials and Ingredients

- muffin wrappers
- muffin pans
- 1 egg
- stirring utensil
- ¾ cup milk
- ½ cup canned pumpkin
- ½ cup raisins
- ½ cup vegetable oil
- 2 cups all-purpose flour
- 2 tsp. pumpkin pie spice
- ⅓ cup sugar
- 3 teaspoons baking powder
- 1 teaspoon salt

Heat oven to 400 degrees F (200 degrees Celsius). Place muffin wrappers in 12 muffin cups. Beat egg and stir in milk, pumpkin, raisins, and oil. Stir in remaining ingredients all at once just until flour is moistened (batter will be lumpy). Fill muffin cups about ¾ full. Bake until golden brown, about 20 minutes. Immediately remove the muffins from the pan. Makes about one dozen muffins.

Pumpkin Pie

Materials and Ingredients

- pastry for 8-inch one-crust pie
- 1 egg
- 1¼ cups canned pumpkin
- ⅔ cup sugar
- ¼ tsp. salt
- ¾ tsp. ground cinnamon
- ¼ tsp. ground ginger
- ⅛ tsp. ground cloves
- 1¼ cups evaporated milk
- knife

Heat oven to 400 degrees Fahrenheit (200 degrees Celsius). Prepare pastry. Beat egg. Beat in remaining ingredients. Pour into pie pan. Bake 15 minutes. Reduce temperature to 350 degrees Fahrenheit (190 degrees Celsius). Bake until knife inserted in center comes out clean (about 35 more minutes.)

The Gingerbread Man

Run, run
As fast as you can.
You can't catch me,
I'm the Gingerbread Man!

Here comes the old woman
And the old man.
Run, run
As fast as you can.

Here comes a pig,
Mr. Gingerbread Man.
Run, run
As fast as you can.

Here comes a dog,
Mr. Gingerbread Man.
Run, run
As fast as you can.

Here comes a horse,
Mr. Gingerbread Man.
Run, run
As fast as you can.

Here comes a cow,
Mr. Gingerbread Man.
Run, run
As fast as you can.

Run, run
As fast as you can.
But the fox caught you,
Mr. Gingerbread Man!

36

The Gingerbread Man Lesson Plans

Week One

1. Begin the unit by asking students about their favorite cookies. Name different kinds of cookies. Have the students vote for their favorites. Encourage students to look around to see how many other students like the same cookies they do. Explain to the students that you are going to read a story about a cookie. Ask them to imagine their favorite cookie talking. Tell them that the cookie in this story can talk!

2. Prior to the lesson, copy the poem "The Gingerbread Man" (see page 36) on a sheet of chart paper. Read the story aloud to the students. Encourage students to join in on the repetitive parts of the story. After finishing the story, ask students to help you identify the characters in the story. Read the story again and determine whether or not all characters were included.

3. Distribute copies of the "The Gingerbread Man" little book. Have students color the pages of the book, cut them out, and staple them together. Pair students with partners and have them read their little books together.

4. Discuss the letter sounds of short *a, f* and *x*. Introduce the sounds that these letters make. Explain to students that sometimes these letters can be found at the beginning, in the middle or at the end of words. Help students locate words that have these letters in their "The Gingerbread Man" little books. Have them complete page 42 for reinforcement of these sounds.

Week Two

1. Read "The Gingerbread Man" aloud to students. Have students follow along in their little books. Point to each word as you read it. After reading the story, tell students that you would like them to look for certain words in the story. For example on the title page, have students locate the word *man*. Have students find a specific word on each page. Have students complete the word matching activity on page 43.

2. Discuss the events of the story. Use these questions to generate discussion about the story:

   • What happens in the story?

   • How does the story end?

   • Is it a good ending?

   • What do you think the old man and the old lady in the story think?

   • What character would you like to be in the story? Why?

   Be sure to ask your students comprehension questions that are open ended to get them thinking.

3. Assign certain students to be characters from the story. As you read the story, have the students act out the parts. Next, read a different version of "The Gingerbread Man" (see the bibliography on page 96 for suggestions). Read as many versions as you can find. Discuss the similarities and differences between the stories. Have students vote on their favorite versions.

The Gingerbread Man Lesson Plans (cont.)

Week Three

1. Read the story aloud again to your students while they follow along in their little books. Point to each word as you read the story. Do not say all the words. Point to a word and have the students read it. Allow students to do more and more of the reading each time you read the story.

2. Discuss how the animals in this story seem like people. Can animals really talk like people do? How can we communicate with animals? In the Literacy Journals (see Preparing this Literacy Unit), have students draw pictures of their pets and what they think their pets would say if they could speak.

3. Copy the gingerbread cookie pattern on page 46. Prior to class, trace the gingerbread pattern for each student on tan construction paper or paper grocery bags. Provide students with materials to decorate the gingerbread people. Use these to decorate your classroom.

Week Four

1. Read "The Gingerbread Man" aloud while students follow along in their little books. Review the order of the story. What happens first? What happens next? What happens last? After this discussion, have the students complete page 44. Allow time for students to share their pictures and favorite parts of the story.

2. Bring to school the ingredients and utensils needed to make gingerbread cookies. Model how to make a batch of cookie dough. Allow a few students at a time to assist, using a cookie cutter to make the cookies.

3. Prior to this lesson, make arrangements to take students on a scavenger hunt. As students come in the class, have a note written on the chalkboard, such as:

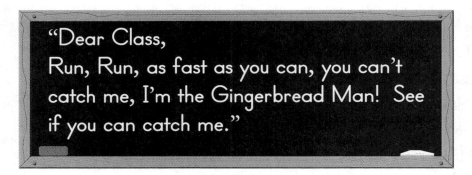

"Dear Class,
Run, Run, as fast as you can, you can't catch me, I'm the Gingerbread Man! See if you can catch me."

Then go to the library to ask the librarian if he or she has seen the Gingerbread Man. The librarian might say he or she saw the Gingerbread Man running to P.E. Go to the gymnasium and ask the P.E. teacher if he or she has seen the Gingerbread Man. Continue to different places in the school in search of the Gingerbread Man. End the scavenger hunt by asking the principal if he or she has seen the Gingerbread Man. The principal should then say that the Gingerbread Man had to go, but he left a treat for the students. The principal then gives each student a gingerbread cookie. Students then take the cookie back to the classroom to decorate and eat. (Use page 45 to organize this activity.)

Literacy in the Works

This page features learning center suggestions that can be used to reinforce skills taught and discussed in the classroom. Select the centers that you think would best meet the needs of your students.

Reading Center

- Set up an area in your room (complete with large beanbags, pillows, and chairs) for independent reading. Keep a shelf of books available at all times for students to read and browse. For this center, have versions of "The Gingerbread Man" available for students to read and compare. (See Bibliography on page 96.)

Art Center

- Make copies of the gingerbread pattern on page 46. Provide colored pencils, crayons, washable markers, watercolor paint, etc. for decorating the patterns. Be sure to have scissors available for students to cut out their gingerbread people. How are these gingerbread people similar and/or different from the gingerbread man in the story? Display these gingerbread people in a prominent place in your classroom.

- Provide a large piece of butcher paper and markers or crayons. Encourage students to design a mural of the events of the story. What happens first? What happens next? Have students work together to design the mural and draw the characters in sequence.

Writing Center

- Provide recipe cards and writing utensils and have students write their own recipes for gingerbread cookies. What ingredients are needed? How much of each ingredient should be used in the recipe? How are they baked? Encourage students to draw pictures to illustrate their recipes.

- Cut index cards into strips and punch a hole in each one. Provide a metal ring for each student. Instruct each student to write words from the story on different strips and put them on his or her metal ring. After the words have been written and added to the ring, instruct students to practice reading their words.

Dramatic Play Center

- Provide costumes and props, such as an apron, a rolling pin, stuffed animals from the story, a cookie sheet, a spatula, etc. Encourage students to work together to act out the story.

Math Center

- Fill a jar with peppermint candies, raisins, or other items commonly used to decorate gingerbread cookies. Have students predict the number of items in the jar and write their predictions on slips of paper. After the predictions have been made, count the contents of the jar with the whole class present.

The Gingerbread Man

1

I'm the
Gingerbread Man.
You can't catch me! 2

Here comes the
old woman, and
the old man.
Mr. Gingerbread Man,
run, run, run. 3

Here comes a pig
and a dog.
Mr. Gingerbread Man,
run, run. 4

Making the Little Book (cont.)

**Here comes a horse and a cow.
Mr. Gingerbread Man, run, run, run.** 5

You can't catch me, I'm the Gingerbread Man. 6

Run, run, as fast as you can! 7

But the fox caught you, Mr. Gingerbread Man! 8

Letters and Sounds

Three of the letters found in "The Gingerbread Man" are short *a*, *f*, and *x*. Write each letter two times. Then draw a picture of something that has that letter sound in it.

| a = m<u>a</u>n | f = <u>f</u>ast | x = fo<u>x</u> |

a

_____
- - - - - - - - - - - - - - - -
_____

a

_____
- - - - - - - - - - - - - - - -
_____

f

_____
- - - - - - - - - - - - - - - -
_____

f

_____
- - - - - - - - - - - - - - - -
_____

x

_____
- - - - - - - - - - - - - - - -
_____

x

_____
- - - - - - - - - - - - - - - -
_____

Word Matching

Can you match the picture with the word? Draw a line from the picture to the word and then write the word on the line.

1. man

_____

_____

3. cow

_____

_____

2. ran

_____

_____

4. woman

_____

_____

5. fox

_____

_____

Now can you find these words in the story?

What Happened First?

Look at the pictures from "The Gingerbread Man" story below. Write the number 1 under the picture showing what happens first. Write the number 2 under the picture that shows what happens second and a 3 under the picture that shows what happens last.

_____   _____   _____

Draw your favorite part of "The Gingerbread Man" in the box below. Try writing a sentence from that part of the story.

Glorious Gingerbread

Gingerbread people can be used to help celebrate the holidays. Use the parent note at the bottom of the page to organize the gingerbread man activity in your classroom. You may want to have parent volunteers on this exciting and busy day.

Materials

- gingerbread cookies
- plates
- graham crackers
- frosting
- variety of candy
- plastic knives

Directions

1. Give each student a gingerbread cookie and a plate to make a gingerbread man or woman.
2. Have students use the frosting and a plastic knife to frost the cookie.
3. Then have students decorate the cookies with raisins and candies.

Dear Parents,

We have been reading "The Gingerbread Man" in our class.

We will be making gingerbread people in our classroom. Please let me know if you are able to donate the materials marked below for this activity:

_____ 1 box graham crackers   _____ 1 can white frosting

_____ 1 bag red hot candies   _____ 1 bag licorice

_____ 1 bag M&Ms   _____ 1 bag spice drops

_____ raisins   _____ 1 bag powdered sugar

_____ 1 package paper plates   _____ 1 package of plastic knives

We will need our supplies by _____.

We will be doing this activity on _____ at _____.
                                             (date)   (time)

Sincerely,

_____

. . . .

_____ Yes! I can send the item checked above.

_____ Yes! I can assist in the classroom.

_____ No, I cannot help at this time.

Jack and Jill

Jack and Jill

Went up a hill,

To fetch a pail of water.

Jack fell down,

And broke his crown,

And Jill came tumbling after.

Personal Safety Rules

- Know your address and phone number.

- Never get into a stranger's car.

- Always wear a seat belt while riding in a car.

- Cross a busy street with a grown-up.

- Tie your shoes so you don't trip on your laces.

Jack and Jill Lesson Plans

Week One

1. Ask students if any of them are wearing bandages. Explain that you have a story about a little boy and a little girl who had an accident. Write the "Jack and Jill" poem on page 47 on chart paper and display it for the students.

2. Read the poem "Jack and Jill." After you have read the poem, encourage the students to read it with you. Point to each word as you read it.

3. Discuss the vocabulary in this poem. Read the poem again, but pause when you come to uncommon words, such as *fetch*, *pail*, and *crown*. Encourage the students to determine the meanings of the words based on the way they are used in the poem.

4. Discuss the letters *j*, *w*, and *d*. Introduce the sounds that these letters make. Explain to students that sometimes these sounds are found at the beginning, the middle, or at the end of a word. Using the chart of the poem, have students locate words that have these letters in them, such as *Jack*, *Jill*, *went*, and *down*. Encourage students to share other words not found in the story that contain these letters. Have students complete page 53.

Week Two

1. Distribute copies of the "Jack and Jill" little book. Have students color the pages, cut them out, and staple their books together. Pair students with partners and have them read their little books together.

2. Read "Jack and Jill" aloud to students. Have them follow along in their little books. Point to each word as you read it. After reading the story, have students look for words. Write the word up on the chalkboard and ask students to find and point to it. Have them look for other words, such as *Jack*, *Jill*, *hill*, *down*, *tumbling*, *after*, *crown*, *pail*, and *fetch*. Have the students complete page 54.

4. Read the poem "Jack and Jill" again with your class. Encourage your class to follow along. Read the poem using a high voice. Now try reading the poem using a low voice, a silly voice, or a shy voice. Invite students to read in their favorite voices. You can also vary this activity by creating a rhythm by tapping or clapping to the beat of the poem. Clap your hands, tap your head, tap your belly, and then tap your arm, your leg, your elbow, etc. Emphasize the rhythm and keep repeating it so that it is easy for your students to follow along.

5. Check the comprehension of the students by playing the beanbag game. Have your students sit in a circle. Ask a question about the poem and then toss a small beanbag to a student. The student who catches the beanbag answers the question. The student tosses the beanbag to a classmate as you ask another question and so on.

Jack and Jill Lesson Plans (cont.)

Week Three

1. Read "Jack and Jill" with the students using their little books. Next time, allow students to read aloud different pages while the other students follow along.

2. Write the "Jack and Jill" poem on sentence strips. Post the sentence strips out of order on the chalkboard. Have students assist you in placing the strips in order. Read the sentences again to check the sequence.

3. Prior to this lesson, write questions that can be answered about the poem on strips of paper. Have the students take turns selecting strips of paper and answering questions, such as:

   - Why are Jack and Jill getting water?

   - What do you think causes Jack to fall?

   - Why do you think Jill comes tumbling after?

   - Where were they going to get water?

4. Point out the opposites in the poem. *Jack* and *Jill* are opposites because Jack is a boy and Jill is a girl. *Up* and *down* are opposites. First Jack and Jill went up the hill and then they came falling down. Ask students to suggest other examples of opposites. Then have students complete page 55.

5. Discuss the importance of following safety rules. Review the safety rules at the bottom of page 47. Are there any that need to be added? Next, create a cover for a class big book entitled, "We Need to Be Safe!" Have students make illustrations depicting what they can do to be safe. Bind all of the pages together to make a big book.

Week Four

1. Read other stories that contain opposites. (See the bibliography on page 96.) Go on a scavenger hunt in search of opposites in your classroom, on the playground, and around the school.

2. Read "Jack and Jill" again and then go outside for a water relay. Divide your class into groups of four or five and have each group stand in a line. Place a pail of water at one end of each line and an empty pail at the other end. Students use cups to scoop the water and pass them down the lines. The passing of water continues until it gets to the last person in line. This person pours the contents of his or her cup into the empty pail. The first team to fill the empty pail is the winner.

3. As a concluding activity, have students work with partners to color and cut out the puppet patterns on page 56. The students then glue the puppets to craft sticks. Allow time for students to practice creating puppet shows. Set up a time for parents or another class to come and watch the puppet shows.

Literacy in the Works

This page features learning center suggestions that can be used to reinforce skills. Select the centers that you think would best meet the needs of your students.

Reading Center

- Write lines from "Jack and Jill" on different sentence strips. Have students work together to read the sentences and determine their correct sequence. Have a little book of this story available for students to check their work.

- Display nonfiction books, magazine articles, and posters about being safe. Have students browse these materials to learn more about safety. Arrange a time in the day to have students report to the class about what they have learned about being safe.

- Set up an area in your room (complete with large beanbags, pillows, and chairs) for independent reading. Keep a shelf of books available at all times for students to read and browse. For this center, have versions of nursery rhymes available for students to read and compare. (See the bibliography on page 96.)

Writing Center

- Ask each student to write about an experience he or she has had that is similar to that of Jack and Jill. Then have the student illustrate the experience to provide more details.

- Select a letter (*j*, *w*, *d*) for students to work on. Ask students to look through magazines and locate pictures that begin with this particular letter. The students can glue these pictures onto construction paper or in pre-assembled little books.

- Provide dough at the center and have students use it to form words from the poem. Be sure to have the "Jack and Jill" poem posted for student reference. Students may also practice making the featured letters for this unit.

Art Center

- Have students color pictures of "Jack and Jill." When they have finished, cut the pictures into large puzzle pieces. Ask the students to put their puzzles back together again. Store the puzzles in envelopes to keep the pieces together.

Math Center

- Have students estimate how many cups of water will fill a pail of water. After you have recorded their estimations, have them determine the answer.

Dramatic Play Center

- Make the puppets on page 56 available for students to use at this center. You may also choose to have props available such as a pail, a hat, a bonnet, an apron, or other items to represent Jack, Jill, the pail, and the well.

Jack and Jill

1

Jack and Jill

2

went up a hill,

3

to fetch a pail of water.

4

Making the Little Book (cont.)

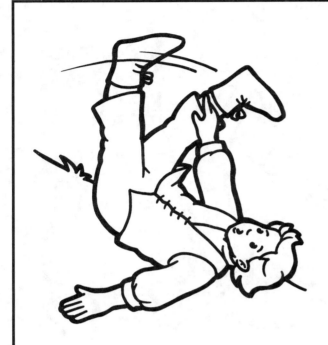

Jack fell down,   5

and broke his crown 6

and Jill came tumbling after.   7

The End

8

Letters and Sounds

Write each letter two times. Then draw a picture of something that has that letter in it.

j = <u>J</u>ack   w = <u>w</u>ent   d = <u>d</u>own

j   j

_____   _____
- - - - - - - - - -   - - - - - - - - - -
_____   _____

w   w

_____   _____
- - - - - - - - - -   - - - - - - - - - -
_____   _____

d   d

_____   _____
- - - - - - - - - -   - - - - - - - - - -
_____   _____

Word Matching

These words come from the poem "Jack and Jill." Write each word. Then write a sentence using the word. Draw a picture that goes with the sentence.

1. down

2. up

3. Jack

4. went

5. Jill

Opposites

Can you match the opposites? Draw a line from each picture to its opposite.

empty

out

in

down

back

full

up

front

See pages 49 and 50 for suggested activities.

The Three Bears

Three furry bears,
A nice family.
Papa and Mama
And baby makes three.

Three furry bears
Went for a walk.
Look out bears,
Here comes Goldilocks!

Three breakfast bowls
Filled with porridge sweet.
Goldilocks is hungry
For something to eat.

Three nice chairs,
A place to sit down.
Goldilocks broke the little one
And fell on the ground.

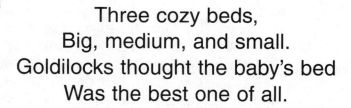

Three cozy beds,
Big, medium, and small.
Goldilocks thought the baby's bed
Was the best one of all.

Three furry bears
Open up the door.
The porridge is all gone;
The chair is on the floor.

Three furry bears
Find Goldilocks at last.
Run, run, run.
Run home fast!

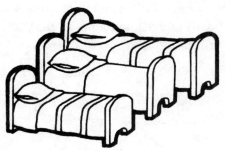
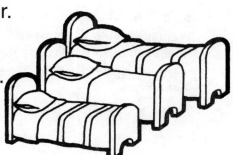

The Three Bears Lesson Plans

Week One

1. Ask students if they have ever seen a bear. Allow time for the students to share experiences they have had seeing bears at zoos, parks, or on television. Ask several questions, such as:

   - How big is a bear?
   - Does a bear have fur?
   - Where do bears live?
   - What do bears eat?

   Tell students that you will read a poem about three make-believe bears and a little girl.

2. Read the poem "The Three Bears." You may want to write the poem on chart paper to display for the children. Ask the students if they have ever heard a story like this poem. Most students will be able to tell you it is like the story, *Goldilocks and the Three Bears*.

3. Read the poem again. When finished, ask students to name the characters as you list them on the chalkboard. Discuss each character. Have students describe and discuss each character's intentions. Who is Goldilocks? Why is she there? What is she doing wrong?

4. On the chalkboard, draw three columns. In the first column, record all the information that students already know about bears. In the second column, record questions they have about bears. Next, read a nonfiction book about bears. (See the bibliography page 96 for suggestions.) In the last column, record information the students learned about bears. You may choose to have students continue to add to this column in future lessons. Point out that the bears in this story are make-believe. Using a Venn diagram, have students compare real bears with make-believe bears. Record differences in the outer circles. Record similarities in the area where the two circles overlap.

Week Two

1. Discuss the sounds of the letters *b* and *z*. Introduce the sounds that these letters make. Explain that sometimes these sounds are found at the beginning, in the middle, or at the end of a word. Write the poem on page 57 on chart paper and have the students locate words that have these letters in them, such as *bears*, *baby*, *breakfast*, *bowls*, *best*, *big*, *broke*, and *cozy*. Encourage students to share other words not found in the story that contain these letter sounds. Have students complete page 63 for reinforcement.

2. Distribute copies of the "The Three Bears" little book. Have students color and cut out the pages and staple them together. Pair students with partners and have them read their little books together.

3. Read "The Three Bears." Have students follow along in their little books. After reading the story, have students look for words. Write the word *bear* on the chalkboard and ask students to find and point to the word. Have students find the following words, as well: *Goldilocks*, *chairs*, *beds*, *porridge*, *hungry*, *fast*. Have students complete page 64.

The Three Bears Lesson Plans *(cont.)*

Week Three

1. Create a story map of the poem with students. What happens first? What happens next? Pair students with partners to create story maps together and have them illustrate their work. Be sure to allow time for students to share their maps with the class. Discuss the different ways to create the map using the same story.

2. Read "The Three Bears" aloud. Next, read a different version of *Goldilocks and the Three Bears*. (See the bibliography on page 96.) Discuss the similarities and differences between the stories. Ask students if these stories are real or make-believe. Have them complete page 65 to determine which animals are real and which are make-believe.

3. Write lines of the story on different sentence strips. Post the sentence strips out of order on the chalkboard. Have students assist you in placing the strips in order. Read the sentences again to check the sequence. Make changes as needed.

4. Read the story again with the students while they follow along in their little books. Point to each word as you read it, but this time, do not say all the words. Point to a word without reading it and have students read it.

5. As an art activity, have each student design a puppet to represent one of the characters in the story. Provide students with paper bags, markers, construction paper, scissors, and glue to make their puppets. When the puppets are finished, have students work in small groups to act out the story of the three little bears.

Week Four

1. Display several nonfiction books about bears. Allow time for students to browse through the books, gathering information about bears. Encourage students to share their findings verbally, by painting pictures, or in other ways.

2. Schedule a day for students to bring their own teddy bears to school. (Be sure to have some extra teddy bears available in case some students do not own teddy bears.) Use the bears for a variety of lessons. Have the children classify, compare and contrast, write stories about them, take them on a teddy bear picnic, etc. Use the teddy bears as assistants for students to report to the class what they have learned about bears. The teddy bears can also be used as props in acting out "The Three Bears."

3. To check comprehension of what your students have learned in this unit, play roll-the-ball. Have your class sit in a large circle. Ask a question about bears, or about "The Three Bears" story. Roll a ball to a student and have him or her answer the question. The child then rolls the ball back to you. Ask another question and roll the ball again.

Literacy in the Works

This page provides learning center suggestions that can be used to reinforce skills. Select the centers that you think would best meet the needs of your students.

Reading Center

- Write the lines from "The Three Bears" on different sentence strips. At this center, have students work together to read the sentences and determine the correct sequence. Have a little book of this story available for students to check their work.

- Set up a "cave" in your room for independent reading. Drape a blanket across the top of chairs or bookshelves. Place large beanbags, pillows, or chairs inside the cave for more comfort. Keep a shelf of books available for students to read and browse. For this center, have versions of *Goldilocks and the Three Bears* available for students to read and compare. You might also want to have nonfiction books available about bears.

Writing Center

- Provide paper and writing utensils for students to write letters to or draw pictures of characters in the story. Students may choose to write letters to one of the bears or to Goldilocks. When finished, have each student place his or her letter in an envelope and attach a sticker to it for a stamp. Read letters to the class at a later time.

Art Center

- Set up an easel with paper. Have students use watercolors to paint pictures of the three bears or other scenes from the story. Display the illustrations around the room. As an additional activity, have students sequence the illustrations by placing them in order according to the scenes.

Science Center

- Display nonfiction books, magazine articles, and posters about bears. Have students browse these materials to learn more about them. Schedule a time to have students report their findings.

Math Center

- Provide gummy bears, crayons, and graph paper. Have each student take a handful of gummy bears to graph. How many red bears? How many yellow bears? How many green bears? Assist students with coloring the graph paper to show the number of bears in each color group.

Dramatic Play Center

- Set up a playhouse area and encourage the children to reenact the story of the three bears. Provide three chairs, three bowls, a small table, three spoons, a pot, and three blankets (for beds) at the center.

Making the Little Book

The Three Bears

1

Papa, Mama, and Baby Bear, that makes three in this brown bear family. 2

Waiting for the porridge, they went for a walk. 3

Look out bears, 'cause here comes Goldilocks. 4

Making the Little Book (cont.)

Goldilocks is hungry, she eats the porridge sweet. 5

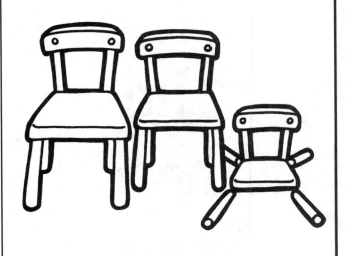

Goldilocks sits and breaks the baby's seat. 6

Goldilocks is tired and she begins to snore. 7

The bears find Goldilocks and she runs out the door. 8

Letters and Sounds

Write each letter two times and then draw a picture of something that has that letter sound in it.

b = <u>b</u>ears   z = co<u>z</u>y

b

b

z

z

b

z

Word Matching

Read each word and then write it. Circle the picture that goes with the word.

1. bear _____

2. bed _____

3. cozy _____

4. broke _____

5. bowl _____

64

Real or Make-Believe?

Look at the pictures below. Do the pictures show bears doing real or make-believe things? Draw a circle around each bear that is doing something a real bear would do. Draw an X on each bear doing something make-believe.

1.

2.

3

4.

5

6.

Draw a picture of an animal that is doing something make-believe. Share your silly picture with your classmates.

The Little Red Hen

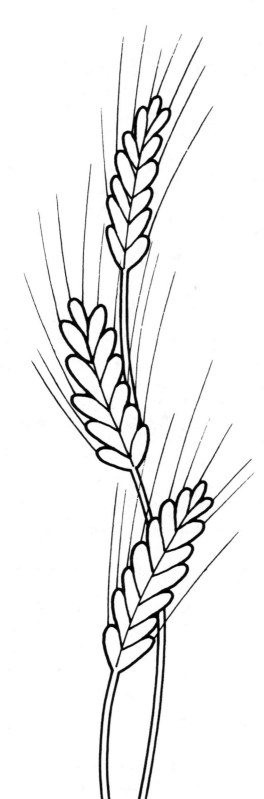

Little Red Hen has found some wheat.
"Who will help me plant the wheat,
so we may have some bread to eat?"
"Not I!" "Not I!" "Not I!"

"Who will help me water the wheat,
so we may have some bread to eat?"
"Not I!" "Not I!" "Not I!"

"Who will help me hoe the wheat,
so we may have some bread to eat?"
"Not I!" "Not I!" "Not I!"

"Who will help me cut the wheat,
so we may have some bread to eat?"
"Not I!" "Not I!" "Not I!"

"Who will help me grind the wheat,
so we may have some bread to eat?"
"Not I!" "Not I!" "Not I!"

"Who will help me make the bread?"
"Not I!" "Not I!" "Not I!"
her friends all said.

Her friends all wanted bread to eat.
But Little Red Hen ate the whole treat!

66

The Little Red Hen Lesson Plans

Week One

1. If possible, use a puppet of a hen to read this poem. You can make a hen puppet of your own using a paper sack or a sock. Read "The Little Red Hen" (page 66) to your class. As you read the story aloud, add expression to the "Not I!" parts of the story. Encourage your students to join in.

2. Discuss the story with the students. Ask questions, such as:

   • Is this a real or make-believe story? How can you tell?

   • What do you think the animal friends should have done?

   • Have you ever grown something in a garden?

   • What kind of help do you need when you plant a garden?

3. Read the poem again. This time have students dramatize the actions, such as planting, watering, hoeing, cutting, grinding, making the bread, and eating. Discuss action words with your students. Invite one student at a time to dramatize a word and have the rest of the class guess the word. Give all students a turn to think of an action word to act out.

4. Write the lines of the story on different sentence strips and use a pocket chart to practice sequencing skills. Have the students place the sentence strips in order. Next, mix up the strips and distribute them to students. Invite students to put their sentence strips in the correct sequence. Place the strips and the pocket chart at your reading center for independent reading practice.

Week Two

1. Discuss the sounds of the letters *r*, short *e*, and *n*. Explain that sometimes these sounds are found at the beginning, in the middle, or at the end of a word. Write the words of the story on chart paper and have students locate words that have these letters in them, such as *red*, *hen*, *her*, *not*, *water*, *grind*, and *bread*. Encourage students to share other words not found in the story that contain these letter sounds. Have students complete page 72 for reinforcement.

2. Distribute copies of the "The Little Red Hen" little book. Have the students color and cut out the pages, and staple them together. Pair students with partners and have them read their little books together.

3. Read "The Little Red Hen" aloud. Have the students follow along in their little books. Point to each word as you read it. Write the word *hen* on the chalkboard and ask students to find and point to it. Have them find other words, such as *little*, *bread*, *eat*, *not*, *I*, *water*, *hoe*, *cut*, *grind*, *make*, and *friends*. Have students complete page 73.

4. Have each child plant a seed in a disposable cup. You may want to have students plant grass seed or birdseed. Water the seeds and place them in a sunny location in your classroom. Have students check the progress of their seeds each day.

The Little Red Hen Lesson Plans (cont.)

Week Three

1. Have students retell the story of the little red hen to check comprehension. Have them dramatize certain parts of the story and ask classmates to guess what they are doing.

2. Read "The Little Red Hen" to the students. Now read a different version of the story (see the bibliography on page 96). Discuss the similarities and differences between the stories. Make a chart to compare the stories. Compare the characters. Who helps and who does not help? Who eats the bread, etc.?

3. Discuss the importance of helping others. Discuss, as a class, how each student can be helpful. Assign helpers with specific jobs, such passing out papers, feeding class pets, being line leaders, and taking messages to the office. Make sure that every student helps in some way. Duplicate the helping hands on page 75 and write the students names' on them. Have students color and cut them out. Make a chart with the class jobs listed and place the student hands beside their assigned jobs.

4. Read the story again as the students follow along in their little books. Point to each word as you read it, but this time, do not say all the words. Point to a word without reading it and have students read it.

5. Invite helpers from your community, such as police officers, doctors, firefighters, nurses, librarians, store clerks, and crossing guards to be guest speakers in your class. Have them discuss the ways they help the community. What would happen if these people weren't there to help or decided not to do their jobs?

Week Four

1. Display several nonfiction books about farm animals. Allow time for students to browse through the books and gather many facts. Have students share their findings.

2. Read a story to students about another hen. As you read the story, frequently pause and ask students to predict what they think might happen next. This activity gets students thinking ahead to different possibilities. Have students complete the activity on page 74.

3. As a culminating activity, have students work in small groups to act out the story "The Little Red Hen." Assign roles to the students. You will need to select one or two students in each group to be narrators. They can read the story from chart paper or from their little books. Allow time for students to practice and prepare their presentations. Set aside a time for the performances and invite another class to watch.

Literacy in the Works

This page provides learning center suggestions that can be used to reinforce skills. Select the centers that you think would best meet the needs of your students.

Writing Center

- Provide dried wheat at this center along with paper and pencil. Have students look at the wheat and write a poem, a story, or ideas that they have about wheat. What can be done with it? What does wheat smell like? What does wheat look like? What does wheat remind you of? What are the uses of wheat?

Art Center

- Set up an easel with paper. Have students use watercolors to paint pictures of the Little Red Hen eating her bread all alone. Ask them to paint the animal friends in the background watching her eat the bread. Are these animals happy or sad? Display the illustrations around the room. Use these paintings as decorations for skit performances.

- Have the children use paper plates and construction-paper scraps to create masks depicting the characters. Staple masks to wooden sticks to hold during skits.

Reading Center

- Write the lines of the story on different sentence strips. At this center, have students work together to read the sentences and determine the correct sequence. Have a little book of this story available for students to check their work.

- Have several versions of *The Little Red Hen* for students to browse on their own. Provide chairs, large beanbags, or pillows to make the reading area more comfortable. Also display the story on chart paper for students to point to and read.

Science Center

- Make mini-books to use as science journals. Have students draw day-by-day pictures of what their seed plantings look like. Have students track the plants' growth. How much water did the plants need? How much sun did the plants get? Are the plants growing?

Math Center

- Put wheat grains into a glass jar for the students to estimate how many grains the jar contains. Place 10 grains on a paper plate so students can get a general idea of how much room 10 grains of wheat take. Have the students practice counting by tens to make their estimations. When all students have made their estimations, divide the grains of wheat into groups of ten. As a class, count by tens to determine how many grains of wheat were in the jar.

Dramatic Play Center

- Provide a variety of kitchen and gardening supplies for children to use in pretending to grow wheat and make bread. Items for the center might include a rake, hoe, watering can, wheelbarrow, sack, apron, mixing bowl, spoons, and a bread pan. Review safety with use of the equipment.

The Little Red Hen

1

The Little Red Hen has found some wheat.

2

Who will help me plant the wheat? Not I! Not I! Not I! 3

Who will help me water the wheat? Not I! Not I! Not I! 4

Making the Little Book (cont.)

Who will help me cut the wheat? Not I! Not I! Not I! 5

Who will help me grind the wheat? Not I! Not I! Not I! 6

Who will help me make the bread? Not I! Not I! Not I! 7

Her friends all wanted some bread to eat, but Little Red Hen ate the whole treat! 8

Letters and Sounds

Write each letter two times and then draw a picture of something that has that letter in it.

r = <u>r</u>ed   n = <u>n</u>ot   e = h<u>e</u>n

r   r

n   n

e   e

Word Matching

Read each word. Then write the word. Draw a picture that goes with the word.

1. red

2. wheat

3. plant

4. hoe

5. hen

Making Predictions

Look at each picture on the left. Draw a line to the picture on the right that shows what will happen next.

Helping Hands

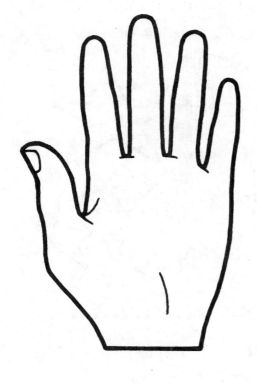

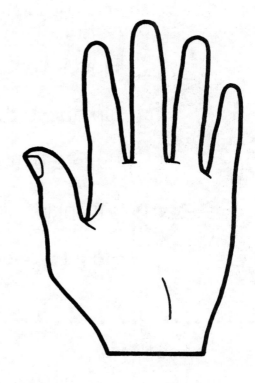

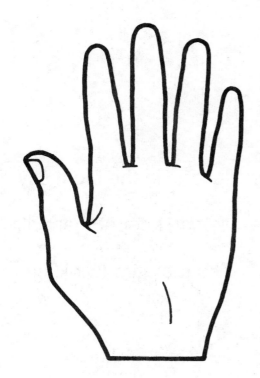

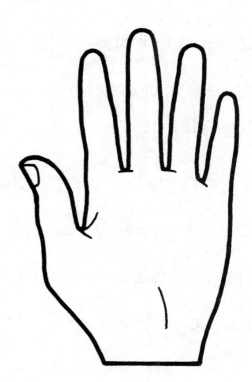

Twinkle, Twinkle, Little Star

Twinkle, twinkle, little star,

How I wonder what you are.

Up above the world so high,

Like a diamond, in the sky.

Twinkle, twinkle, little star,

How I wonder what you are.

What Is a Star?

• A star is a ball of gas.

• Stars are millions of miles away.

• The sun is a star.

• Groups of stars make pictures or constellations in the night sky.

• There are so many stars in the sky that we can't count them all.

• Stars don't really twinkle. They just look like they are twinkling.

• Stars are very hot.

Twinkle, Twinkle, Little Star Lesson Plans

Week One

1. Ask the children if they have ever wished upon a star. What did they wish for? Did the wish come true? Why do they think people wish on stars? Read the poem, "Twinkle, Twinkle, Little Star." You might want to write the poem (page 76) on chart paper to use for this activity.

2. Hold up several objects and ask the students to describe them by comparing each one to another object. For example, an orange is like a ball. Draw students' attention to the line in the poem that reads, "like a diamond in the sky," and ask them to guess what the diamond is being compared to. Make sentence strips using statements such as:

   - The moon is like a . . .
   - The earth is like a . . .
   - School is like . . .
   - The sun is like a . . .

   Ask students to offer suggestions to complete the sentences. Instruct each child to copy one of the sentences and illustrate it. Display their finished projects around the classroom or in a class book.

3. Ask students what they think it would be like in outer space. How would life be different? What would it look like on the moon? What would a star look like up close? What else is in the sky? Talk about astronauts. Discuss *far* and *near* and make a class list of things that are close to us and far away.

4. Prior to reading the poem again, cover up words with paper. Use a cloze technique by asking students to name the missing words.

Week Two

1. Discuss the sounds of letters *t*, short *u*, and *y*. Explain to students that sometimes these sounds are found at the beginning, in the middle, or at the end of a word. Write the story on chart paper and have students locate words that have these letters in them, such as *twinkle*, *you*, and *up*. Encourage students to share other words not found in the story that contain these letters. Have your students complete page 82 for reinforcement.

2. Distribute copies of the little book for "Twinkle, Twinkle, Little Star." Have students color and cut out the pages and staple their books together. Pair students with partners and have them read their little books together. Use a variety of methods to read the little book with your students, such as echo reading (you read a line and the students echo back), buddy reading, or even clapping a rhythm while reading.

3. Read "Twinkle, Twinkle, Little Star." Have students follow along in their little books. Write the word *star* on the chalkboard and ask them to find and point to the word. Have them find other words, such as *twinkle*, *little*, *up*, *above*, *diamond*, *sky*, *high*, and *like*. Have students complete page 83.

Twinkle, Twinkle, Little Star Lesson Plans *(cont.)*

Week Three

1. Read "Twinkle, Twinkle, Little Star" to the students. Now read a different story about a star. (See the bibliography on page 96.) Discuss the similarities and differences between the stories. Explain to the children that it is important to look for details in stories. Have them use page 84 to determine the details from the little book.

2. As an art activity, supply students with yellow construction paper, scissors, a star pattern, glitter, and glue to have students make their own stars. Have each child trace a star onto construction paper. The child cuts out the star and then, with adult help, glues glitter on to the star.

3. In the poem, the star is compared to a diamond. Have a scavenger hunt around your classroom or in the school, looking for objects that are diamond-shaped.

Week Four

1. Display several nonfiction books on stars. Allow time for students to browse through the books to gather facts. Make a list of facts that students have found. Use the bottom of page 76 as a reference for more star facts.

2. On the chalkboard write *A star is* . . . . Then have each student copy these words and add an ending to the sentence. Have each student make an illustration to accompany the sentence. Bind student pages together to create a book. Make a cover for the book and store it in the class library.

3. Discuss space travel. Duplicate page 85 for students and have them color and cut out either the girl or the boy astronaut. Have each child paste the picture onto a piece of blank paper and then illustrate the rest of the picture in the space surrounding the astronaut. What is the astronaut doing? Pair students with buddies to share their pictures.

4. To check comprehension, play Roll-the-Ball. Have the children sit in a large circle. Ask a question about stars or the "Twinkle, Twinkle, Little Star" poem. Roll the ball to a student and have him or her answer the question. He or she then rolls the ball back to you. Ask another question and roll the ball again to another student.

Literacy in the Works

This page provides learning center suggestions that can be used to reinforce skills taught and discussed in the classroom. Select the centers that you think would best meet the needs of your students.

Writing Center

- Provide play dough for students to use to spell words from the poem. Be sure to have the "Twinkle, Twinkle, Little Star" poem posted for student reference. Students may also practice making the featured letters for this unit.

- Ask each student to write about an experience he or she has had at night while looking at the night sky. Have the student write as many words as he or she can about the incident. Then have each student illustrate the experience to provide more details.

- Select a letter of focus from this unit (*t*, *u*, and *y*) for students to work on. Have students write this letter on sheets of paper. Then ask them to look through magazines and locate pictures that begin with this letter.

Reading Center

- Display sentence strips containing the lines from the "Twinkle, Twinkle, Little Star" poem. At this center, have students work together to read the sentences and determine the sequence of the poem. Provide a little book of this poem for students to check their work.

- Display nonfiction books, magazine articles, and posters about stars. Have students browse these materials to learn more about them. Arrange a time in the day to have students report to the class what they have learned about stars.

- Set up an area in your room (complete with large beanbags, pillows, and chairs) for independent reading. Keep a shelf of books available at all times for students to read and browse. For this center, have a variety of poems and nursery rhymes available for students to read.

Art Center

- Have students color pictures of things they would wish for on a star. When they have finished, cut the pictures into large puzzle pieces. Students can then try to put their puzzles back together again. Store the puzzles in envelopes to keep the pieces organized.

Math Center

- Have students create pictures using stars. Have stars in a variety of sizes to cut out. Each student pastes the stars to paper to make a pattern or uses the stars to create a picture.

Dramatic Play Center

- Provide simple instruments with which students can create a beat as they read or recite "Twinkle, Twinkle, Little Star." Instruments might include spoons to tap together, empty containers to beat like drums, small containers of rice and beans to shake, etc.

Twinkle, Twinkle, Little Star

1

Twinkle, twinkle, little star

2

How I wonder what you are.

3

Up above the world so high,

4

Making the Little Book *(cont.)*

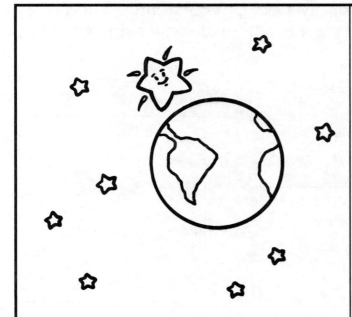

Like a diamond in the sky.   5

Twinkle, twinkle little star,   6

How I wonder what you are!   7

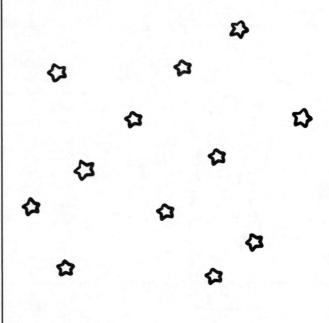

The End   8

Letters and Sounds

Three of the letter sounds found in "Twinkle, Twinkle, Little Star" are *t*, short *u*, and *y*. Write each letter two times. Then draw a picture of something that has that letter sound in it.

t = t̲winkle   u = u̲p   y = y̲ou

t   t

_____   _____
- - - - - - - - - - - - -   - - - - - - - - - - - - -
_____   _____

u   u

_____   _____
- - - - - - - - - - - - -   - - - - - - - - - - - - -
_____   _____

y   y

_____   _____
- - - - - - - - - - - - -   - - - - - - - - - - - - -
_____   _____

Word Matching

These words come from the poem, "Twinkle, Twinkle, Little Star." First read the word, and then write the word. Next, underline the word in the sentence.

1. star _____ The star is big.

2. up _____ He is up there.

3. you _____ I like you.

4. the _____ Here is the cat.

5. sky _____ It's in the sky.

Story Details

Think about the poem "Twinkle, Twinkle, Little Star." Look at each picture.
Color the pictures that show something from the little book.

Astronaut Patterns

Teacher Note: Cut out the blackened part of the helmet to reveal the astronaut's face.

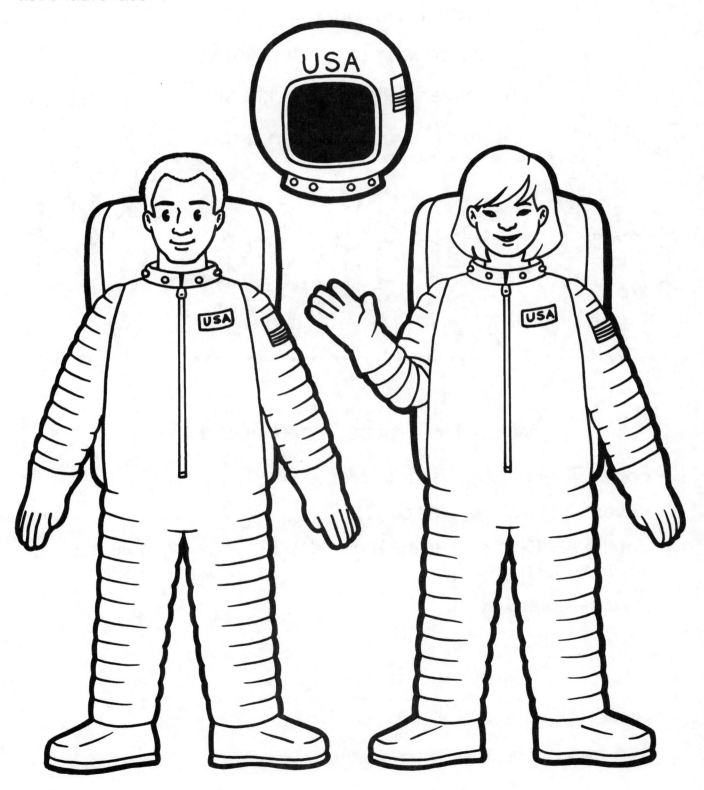

Mary, Mary, Quite Contrary

Mary, Mary, quite contrary,

How does your garden grow?

With silver bells and cockle shells,

And pretty maids all in a row.

What Do These Words Mean?

- **contrary**—grouchy, disagreeable

- **silver bells**—shiny, gray color

- **cockle shell**—a cockle is a mollusk with a shell (such as a scallop shell)

- **maids**—young ladies

Mary, Mary, Quite Contrary Lesson Plans

Week One

1. Ask students if they have ever planted a garden. What was planted in the garden? What did the plants look like? What kind of work goes into a garden? Why are gardens planted? What kinds of food have students eaten from a garden? Make a copy of the poem on page 86.

2. Read the poem "Mary, Mary, Quite Contrary." Discuss the poem with students. Ask the following questions: What is the name of the girl? What did she grow in her garden? Acknowledge that there are some big words in this poem. Invite students to help you identify these words and define them. Read the poem again and make a list of the things Mary grew in her garden. The list will include the words *silver bells*, *cockle shells*, and *maids*. What are these things? Use page 86 as a reference to assist your discussion.

3. Replace new words for the original words in the poem. Read the poem again. Do the new words help in the comprehension of the poem? Discuss the meaning of the word *contrary*. What does it mean when it says that Mary was contrary? Ask what might have made Mary contrary. Talk about feelings and how facial expressions can show how we are feeling. Have children draw four circles and illustrate facial expressions for *happy*, *sad*, *mad*, and *surprised*. When finished, play a game where a student shows an expression and the class members guess the emotion being expressed.

4. Discuss the sounds of the letters *q*, *c*, and *g*. Introduce the sounds that these letters make. Explain to students that sometimes these sounds are found at the beginning, the middle, or the end of a word. Make a chart of page 86 and have students locate words that have these letters in them, such as *quite*, *contrary*, *garden*, *grow*, and *cockle shells*. Encourage students to share other words not found in the story that use these letter sounds. Have them complete page 92 for reinforcement of these letters.

Week Two

1. Distribute copies of the "Mary, Mary, Quite Contrary" little book. Have students color the pages and then cut them out. Help students assemble and staple their books together. Pair students with partners and have them read their little books together.

2. Read "Mary, Mary, Quite Contrary" aloud to students from a little book like theirs. Have students follow along in their little books. Point to each word as you read it. After reading the story, have students look for words. Write the word *garden* on the chalkboard and ask students to find and point to the word. Other words to look for include *Mary*, *quite*, *grow*, *silver*, *bells*, *cockle*, *shells*, *pretty* and *maid*. Discuss how illustrations and pictures can help students locate words. Have students complete page 93 using words from the poem.

Mary, Mary, Quite Contrary Lesson Plans (cont.)

Week Three

1. Have students retell the poem about Mary to check comprehension. Make up statements about the poem that do not exist to see if students can correct you.

2. Invite someone who grows flowers to come to visit your class. If possible, have the grower bring in flowers that resemble shells and bells, and pretty maids (sunflowers). Explain that this is perhaps why the poem uses these comparisons.

3. Read the poem to the students. Ask students to tell you word-for-word the lines from the poem. Write these words on the chalkboard. Next, hold up the poster you have made of this poem and check the students' work. Are the lines and words in correct order? Make changes as needed. Talk with students about the story or poem details. The details of a story or poem can help aid comprehension and understanding. Have students complete page 94 on locating and identifying details.

4. Read the poem again with the students while they follow along in their little books. Point to each word as you read it, but do not say all the words. Point to a word and have students read it.

5. As an art activity, supply students with construction paper, small pieces of tissue paper, and glue sticks. Have students use small pieces of colored tissue paper to design flower gardens. Have them try to make their flowers look like shells and bells. Display the gardens throughout the room for decoration.

Week Four

1. Read other stories with your class about gardens. You can refer to the bibliography on page 96 for a suggestion. Go on a scavenger hunt in search of different types of plants. Take a walk around your school to locate different sizes, different colors, and different textures of plants. Discuss the fact that all plants start from seeds. All seeds need water, soil, and sunlight to grow. Have students complete page 95 about sequencing the growth of a plant.

2. Read "Mary, Mary, Quite Contrary" again. What happened next? Encourage students to brainstorm what might happen after the end of the poem. What happens to Mary and her garden? Have students illustrate their new endings.

3. Plan a day to create a salad of foods that are grown in gardens. You may choose to make a salad with cucumbers, bell peppers (silver bells), carrots, cauliflower (cockle shells), broccoli (pretty maids), and tomatoes. Be creative! Be sure to wash the vegetables and discuss why they need to be washed. Discuss how these living things will help our living bodies grow and be healthy.

Literacy in the Works

This page provides learning center suggestions that can be used to reinforce skills taught and discussed in the classroom. Select the centers that you think would best meet the needs of your students.

Writing Center

- Mary was defined as "contrary" in the poem. How would students define themselves? Have each student draw a self-portrait. Have students use adjectives to describe themselves. Do any of these words rhyme with the students' names like the words Mary and contrary?

- Have each students write a story about Mary. Ask each of them to draw a picture of Mary at school, in the store, or at the park, etc. What does Mary do? What happens? Have pre-constructed blank little books available for students to illustrate their stories. Assist students, as needed, with words and sentences. Be sure to have each student determine a title and cover for his or her book.

Reading Center

- Provide sentence strips with the lines from "Mary, Mary, Quite Contrary." At this center, have students work together to read the sentences and determine the sequence of the poem. Have a little book of this story available for students to check their work.

- Set up an area in your room (complete with large beanbags, pillows, and chairs) for independent reading. Keep a shelf of books available at all times for students to read and browse. For this center, have versions of nursery rhymes available for students to read and compare. You can also have nonfiction books available about gardens.

Art Center

- Plants and flowers are living things. Have students cut out pictures of living and non-living things from magazines. Then give each student a sheet of construction paper to fold in half. On one side of the paper, have students paste pictures of living things. On the other side, have students paste magazine pictures of non-living things.

Science Center

- Display nonfiction books, magazine articles, and/or posters about gardens or plants. Have students browse these materials to learn more about plants.

Math Center

- Have students color a picture of a garden using numbers. On a sheet of paper, ask each student use watercolors to paint the following in their gardens: five trees, four roses, three sunflowers, two tulips, and one daisy. Be sure to have a picture of each type of plant available for students to use as a reference.

Dramatic Play Center

- Set up an area for students to reenact the process of planting a garden. Provide pots, seeds, a hoe, cloth or plastic flowers, and pinto beans to use as dirt.

Mary, Mary, Quite Contrary

1

Mary, Mary 2

quite contrary, 3

How does your garden grow? 4

Making the Little Book (cont.)

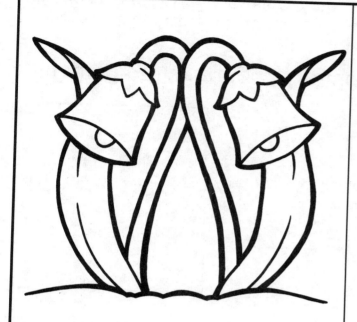

With silver bells   5

and cockle shells,   6

and pretty maids all in a row.   7

The End   8

Letters and Sounds

Three of the letter sounds found in "Mary, Mary, Quite Contrary" are *q*, *c*, and *g*. Write each letter two times and then draw a picture of something that has that letter sound in it.

q = <u>q</u>uite   c = <u>c</u>ontrary   g = <u>g</u>arden

q   q

c   c

g   g

Word Matching

These words come from the poem "Mary, Mary, Quite Contrary." Read and write the word. Circle the picture that goes with the word.

1. garden _____

2. shells _____

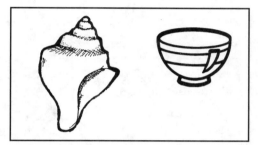

3. grow _____

4. bells _____

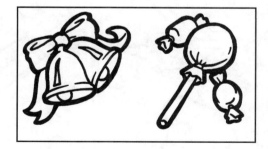

5. row _____

Looking at Details

Look at the pictures in each box below. Circle the picture that does not belong. Verbally tell why it does not belong.

94

Planting a Seed

Color and cut out the pictures. Paste the pictures, in order, on a sheet of construction paper.

Bibliography

Fiction

Brett, Jan. *Gingerbread Baby*. Putnam, 1999.

———. *Goldilocks and the Three Bears*. Dodd, Mead, & Company, 1987.

Carle, Eric. *The Very Busy Spider*. Putnam, 1989.

Cousins, Lucy. *The Lucy Cousins Book of Nursery Rhymes*. Dutton Books, 1999.

Cutts, David. *The Gingerbread Boy*. Troll Associates, 1979.

DeLuise, Dom. *Goldilocks*. Simon Shuster, 1992.

Disalvo-Ryan, Dyanne. *City Green*. Williams, Morrow & Co., 1994.

Eisen, Armand. *Goldilocks and the Three Bears*. Alfred A. Knopf, 1989.

Galdone, Paul. *The Little Red Hen*. Houghton Mifflin, 1973.

———. *The Three Bears*. Clarion Books, 1972.

Graham, Margaret Bloy. *Be Nice to Spiders*. HarperCollins, 1967.

Lin, Grace. *The Ugly Vegetables*. Charlesbridge, 1999.

LynRay, Mary. *Pumpkins: A Story for a Field*. Voyager Books, 1996.

Marshall, James. *Goldilocks and the Three Bears*. Dial Books, 1988.

———. *The Three Little Pigs*. Viking Penguin, 1989.

Morris, Ann. *Bread, Bread, Bread*. Lothrop, 1989.

Opie, Iona Archibald. *My Very First Mother Goose*. Candlewick Press, 1996.

Rounds, Glen. *Three Little Pigs and the Big Bad Wolf*. Holiday House, 1992.

Scarry, Richard. *The Gingerbread Man*. Western Publishing Company, 1975.

Schiller, Pamela. *The Complete Book of Rhymes, Songs, Poems, Finger Plays, and Chants*. Gryphon House, 2002.

Schmidt, Karen. *The Gingerbread Man*. Scholastic, 1967.

———. *The Little Red Hen*. Grosset & Dunlap, 1984.

Scieszka, Jon. *The True Story of the Three Little Pigs*. Penguin Books, 1990.

Trapani, Iza. *Twinkle, Twinkle, Little Star*. Charlesbridge, 1998.

Udry, Janice. *A Tree Is Nice*. Harper, 1987.

Zemach, Margot. *The Little Red Hen*. Farrar, Straus & Giroux, 1983.

———. *The Three Little Pigs*. Farrar, Straus & Giroux, 1988.

Nonfiction

Allen, Judy. *Are You a Spider?* Backyard Books, 2000.

Burckhardt, Ann. *Pumpkins*. Bridgestone Books, 1996.

Greenway, Theresa. *Amazing Bears*. Knopf Books, 1992.

Hoban, Tana. *Push, Pull, Empty, Full: A Book of Opposites*. Macmillan, 1972.

Joyce, Irma. *Never Talk to Strangers: A Book About Personal Safety*. Golden Books, 2000.

Lovejoy, Sharon. *Roots, Shoots, Buckets, and Boots: Gardening Together with Kids*. Workman Publishing, 1999.

Lynch, Wayne. *Bears, Bears, Bears*. Firefly Books, 1995.

Patent, Dorothy. *Bears of the Wild*. Holiday House, 1980.